MW00878278

Visit www.booksurge.com to order additional copies.

It's All in the Blood

The Cleansing, Overcoming, Life-Giving Blood of Jesus

Pastor Leonard Gardner

2008

It's All in the Blood

CONTENTS

The Blood

Life, that mysterious something which scientists have not yet been able to define or fathom, is said by God to be "in the blood" (Leviticus 17:11), which means that there can be no life without blood.

For a deeper understanding of this truth, we look to the Bible, which is the Word of the one and only God, who created the human body and the blood which flows through it. From the Bible, we learn the fundamental truths that have existed eternally in the heart of God. From the beginning to the end of Scripture, from the closing of the gates of Eden to the opening of the gates of the heavenly Zion, a golden thread of "the blood" runs through Scripture. It is "the blood" that unites the beginning and the end, and it is ultimately the blood that gloriously restores what sin had destroyed.

The heart of God has rejoiced in the blood of Jesus, and the human heart will never rest nor find salvation until we too learn to walk and glory in the power of that blood. However, it is not only the repentant sinner, longing for pardon from sin, who must value the blood. The redeemed will also benefit, because God offers us victory, liberty, and power, as well as glorious fellowship with Him and with one another—all because of the blood of Jesus.

Understanding the Blood

When many people think of blood, they typically think of something that is unpleasant or even repulsive. It is not a subject about which we often desire to speak, because it makes us uncomfortable. Some people get light-headed or even faint at the sight of blood. Though blood continuously courses through our bodies, we don't really understand much about it, nor speak about it very often. It is vitally important, yet often ignored.

Likewise, in a spiritual sense, the blood of Jesus is a subject which isn't wholly understood nor preached as often as it should be. In Jesus' blood there is liberty, victory, and power. It is so very important that we recognize and acknowledge the work of the blood, so that people can be set free and liberated in the name of Jesus. Sometimes we struggle in our Christian walk because we don't wholly understand the work of the blood.

The Spirit, the Word, and the Blood

I believe that it is important for the church of Jesus Christ to revisit some of the great truths and principles upon which Christianity is built. These are the truths that have lived on throughout the ages, and which have been the very instruments that have brought victory in the darkest times.

I John 5:7 declares, "For there are three that bear record in heaven, the Father, the Word, and the Holy Ghost; and these three are one." Verse 8 states, "And there are three that bear witness in earth, the Spirit, the water, and the blood, and these three agree in one." The spirit, the water, and the blood bear witness (reveal God's truth and glory) in earth, and they are inseparable and powerful. In the Bible, water represents the Word of God (Ephesians 5:26). Therefore, we understand that the three that bear witness on earth are the Spirit, the Word, and the blood.

First, the Spirit "bears witness" to God's truth and glory. During the last several decades, there has been a great restoration and focus on the Person and work of the Holy Spirit. Many anointed Christian leaders have emphasized the fact that we need a personal relationship with the Person of the Holy Spirit. During the period of time often referred to as "the Charismatic renewal," the things of the Spirit became a focal point, and we spoke of the gifts of the Spirit, the fruit of the Spirit, and life in the Spirit. People began to frequently use the phrase "filled with the Spirit." It seemed that God was breathing the truths of the Spirit afresh.

Secondly, the Word bears witness to God's truth and glory. On the heels of the Charismatic renewal came the witness and revival of the Word of God. There has been a great restoration and focus on the teaching of the Word, the exposition of the Word, and the exegesis of the Word. God has raised up many great Bible teachers over the last several decades. In recent decades, more people have begun to buy Bibles and seriously study them. They've begun to understand the importance of knowing the Word of God in a very intimate and personal way. The Word of God has come alive in a new and fresh way to many people.

The Blood from Genesis to Revelation

The blood is the third element that bears witness to God's glory. I believe that we are going to witness restoration of the revelation of the work of blood of Jesus Christ. The mystery of the blood is going to be manifest, and the power of the blood is going to be more evident. Many people who love Jesus are struggling to live an overcoming, victorious life. They have weaknesses in their lives that they simply can't seem to overcome. I believe we're going to see victory through the revelation of the power of the blood of Jesus Christ.

The blood occupies a very prominent place in the Word of God. You might say the whole Bible is "bounded" by the blood because both the first book and the last book of the Bible (Genesis and Revelation) each speak about the blood.

Genesis 3:21 declares, "Unto Adam also and to his wife did the Lord God make coats of skins, and clothed them." Immediately after Adam and Eve sinned and suddenly realized that they were naked and subsequently felt ashamed, God shed the blood of an innocent animal in order to clothe them. God shed blood in order to literally "cover" them.

Revelation 5:11 declares, "I beheld, and I heard the voice of many angels around the throne and the beasts and the elders; and the number of them was ten thousand times ten thousand <one hundred million>, and thousands of thousands." The multitude was "saying with a loud voice, Worthy is the Lamb that was slain to receive power, and riches, and wisdom, and strength, and honour, and glory, and blessing."

If we are to be saved, it must come by the blood. If we want to live above our fleshly desires, we need to understand the blood. If we want to overcome the enemy, we must apply the blood. I believe that it is the understanding of the blood that ushers us into the place of victorious and liberated living. Please note some of the wonderful things that the blood provides for us:

- *Life*. Leviticus 17:11 declares, "The life is in the blood."
- *Forgiveness*. Hebrews 9:22 declares, "without the shedding of blood there is no forgiveness." (NIV)
- *Justification*. Romans 5:9 states, "Much more then being justified by His blood, we shall be saved from wrath through Him."

- _Redemption_. Ephesians 1:7 and Colossians 1:14 both declare that we are redeemed by the blood of the Lamb.
- _Peace_. Colossians 1:20 states that we have peace with God through His blood.
- _Cleansing_. I John 1:7, declares "if we walk in the light as He is in the light, we have fellowship one with another, and the blood of Jesus Christ his Son cleanseth us from all sin."
- _Sanctification_. Hebrews 13:12 declares that we are sanctified by the blood of Jesus.
- _Protection_. In Exodus 12:13, the Angel of Death passed over the people who applied the blood to the lintel and doorposts of their houses.
- _Overcoming Power_. Revelation 12:11 states that believers overcame the enemy (Satan) by the blood of the Lamb and the word of their testimony.

All of these incredible benefits come to us only through the blood of Jesus. _It's all in His blood!_ In the pages of this book, which is a collection of transcribed teachings which were given by Pastor Leonard Gardner, we will embark on a fascinating journey that will take us to the earliest times in human history, to the torture and crucifixion of Jesus, and also into the inner workings of our physical bodies. Along the way, we will uncover and understand amazing truths regarding the blood of Jesus, and how it can literally transform our lives! I trust that this book will help us to understand in a greater measure the provision that God has made for all of us through the blood of the Lord Jesus Christ.

CHAPTER I

The Life-Giving Blood

The blood of Jesus gives life, bringing to His Body (all believers) everything that is essential for the body to experience health and strength. Leviticus 17:11 declares that "the life of the flesh is in the blood." I am convinced that the Church of Jesus Christ must come into a greater appreciation for the power of the blood, because in that truth is not only the victory that sets _us_ free, but it also overcomes the work of the enemy in _others'_ lives as we minister to them in the name of Jesus.

First the Natural, Then the Spiritual

There is a Biblical principle which states that the knowledge of natural things helps us to understand spiritual things. I Corinthians 15:46 declares, "Howbeit that was not first which is spiritual, but that which is natural; and afterward that which is spiritual." Jesus illustrated this principle by frequently using similes and metaphors which related to _natural_ things in order to teach _spiritual_ concepts.

Similarly, as we examine the spiritual life-giving power of the blood, I think it important to understand how God has designed the human body. Understanding how the _natural_ body works helps us understand how the _spiritual_ body works, how to apply the blood, how to plead the blood, and how to call upon the blood to get the results that God has purposed for the blood to produce.

The Amazing Human Body

The basic unit in the physical body is the cell. A normal healthy adult has approximately one hundred trillion cells in his or her body. Cells come in a variety of shapes depending upon their location and their function in the body, yet they all share the same DNA. Some are shaped like rods, some like discs, and some like spears. Cells also vary in size. Some cells are so small that one million of them could fit on the head of a pin.

It is remarkable that this collection of one hundred trillion cells of varying shapes, sizes, and functions all work together in harmony. Cells with different tasks, living in harmony, minding their own business, and doing their own work. Though each cell is unique and different, it has two things in common with every other cell. First, it needs nourishment. That is, it needs to be fed. Secondly, it produces waste that must be carried away.

One hundred trillion cells of different shapes, sizes, and functions all need to receive nourishment and have their waste carried away. God solved this incredibly complex problem by designing a massive transportation system in the body called the *bloodstream*. Adults have between five and seven quarts of blood in their body. If all the blood vessels in one person's bloodstream were put end to end, they would be sixty thousand miles long. The distance around the earth at the equator is about twenty-five thousand miles. Therefore, if all of one's blood vessels were put end to end they would go two and a half times around the earth.

Recorded in Psalm 139, David effectively said, "I'm going to praise you Lord because I am fearfully and wonderfully made." God has designed the human body so that each of the one hundred trillion cells is within the width of one human hair away from a capillary from which it can receive nourishment.

God took this sixty thousand mile long transportation system called the bloodstream and organized it in such a way that all one hundred trillion cells have access to it. Simply amazing!

Circulating the Blood

God designed and placed a pump called the heart in the body in order to circulate the blood. There isn't an engineer in the world that can build a pump to perform like the one God created and put in our bodies. The heart is the primary organ of the circulatory system and is responsible for the movement of blood through our bodies. It sends the blood to the lungs, where it picks up oxygen and discharges carbon dioxide. The blood then returns to the heart, which propels it through the aorta, the huge main artery. Blood pours through the aorta into a series of arteries that become progressively smaller. It then flows through capillaries, which are the smallest of the vessels and are located throughout the body. The blood travels back from the capillaries up through progressively larger veins until it reaches the heart. Blood makes a "round trip" through the entire body in only twenty seconds. Therefore, it makes an amazing half million trips through the body in four months.

The blood carries the nutrients, such as vitamins, minerals, cobalt, glucose, fats, acids, and hormones, that the cells need in order to live. The cells burn those nutrients as fuel. For example, our eyes have about two hundred fifty million cells. Part of what they receive is sugar. They burn that as fuel, convert it to energy, and send an electrical impulse to the brain. The reason we can blink our eyes in an involuntary motion is because of the energy that's been acquired by burning the nutrients. All of this happens without us consciously thinking about it. This is typical of other functions which are also constantly occurring in our bodies.

Part Grocery Truck / Part Garbage Truck

When cells burn nutrients, waste is one of the by-products of the reaction. Another miraculous facet of the amazing transportation system called the bloodstream is that it also picks up the waste that is given off and carries it away. Imagine a gigantic truck whose front end has all the groceries that could ever be needed, and the back end is a garbage truck. Of course, we know that's not practical for sanitary reasons, but if we overlook that for a moment, we can get an idea of how the bloodstream functions. If such a truck existed, we would only have to stand by the door of our house and simply reach out the door and say, "I'll have some of those groceries, some of that, and some of that." Also, as the truck moves by, we deposit our garbage into it. The truck then comes back around twenty seconds later. We never have to leave the house, because this truck brings everything to us which is needed to sustain life, and takes away all of the garbage. All we do is receive the nourishment, and deposit the waste.

Each of the one hundred trillion cells in our body understands its function and knows what it needs. As the bloodstream flows by, the cells reach out and say, for example, "I'll have some cobalt and some glucose. Acids—no, I don't need any of that. Fats—none of that either." The cells have the ability, authority, and privilege of withdrawing everything they need from the bloodstream. God has designed and created each cell such that it has the intelligence to know what it needs, and He has given it the privilege of withdrawing whatever it needs from the bloodstream.

Every Single Cell Needs the Blood

It is important to note that every single cell in the body is at the mercy of the blood. Cells die without oxygen, and one of the things the bloodstream delivers to the cells is oxygen. We can live several days without water and a few weeks without food, but we can only live a few minutes without oxygen. One of the waste products that the bloodstream carries away from the cells is carbon dioxide. When we are inhaling and exhaling, it isn't an academic exercise; it's absolutely vital. As the blood passes through the lungs, it absorbs oxygen to deliver through the bloodstream to every one of the cells. The blood also picks up the waste (carbon dioxide) from the lungs, to expel from the body when we exhale.

If for some reason the blood doesn't get to the cells, they die. The cells are always dependent upon the blood. The life is in the blood, the nutrients are in the blood, and the expulsion of the poisons and toxins are by way of the blood. The blood, flowing through this transportation system made up of sixty thousand miles of blood vessels, is delivering "the good" and picking up "the bad" in order to keep our cells alive. The blood is simply amazing in its function.

A Controversial Message

Jesus preached a controversial message about the blood that caused many to turn away from Him and no longer follow Him. It is found in John Chapter 6, starting in verse 53, which declares, "Then Jesus said unto them, verily, verily, I say unto you, except you eat the flesh of the Son of man, and drink his blood, you have no life in you." The word translated "life" is the Greek word *zoë*, which refers to "the God kind of life that is both eternal and abundant."

Jesus continued, "Whoso eateth my flesh, and drinketh my blood, hath eternal life; and I will raise him up at the last day. For my flesh is meat indeed, and my blood is drink indeed. He that eateth my flesh, and drinketh my blood, dwelleth in me, and I in him. As the living Father hath sent me, and I live by the Father; so he that eateth me, even he shall live by me."

After Jesus' controversial message, John 6:60 declares, "Many therefore of his disciples, when they had heard this, said, this is a hard saying." Other translations effectively say, "This is tough; this is severe; this is harsh."

Scripture continues, "When Jesus knew in himself that his disciples murmured at it, he said unto them, doth this offend you?" Verse 63 declares, "It is the spirit that quickeneth; the flesh profiteth nothing; the words that I speak unto you, they are spirit, and they are life." Verse 66 states, "From that time many of his disciples went back, and walked no more with him. Then Jesus said unto the twelve, Will ye also go away? Then Simon Peter answered him, Lord, to whom shall we go? Thou hast the words of eternal life. And we believe and are sure that thou art the Christ, the Son of the living God."

Understanding Jesus' Message

If we understand the background, teaching, and education of Jesus' listeners, perhaps we can better appreciate their inability to embrace this message. From the very beginning, dating from the time of Noah, God had given a commandment, "You cannot drink blood." He declared it again through the Levitical priesthood, "You cannot drink blood, because the life is in the blood." If you kill an animal for sacrifice, you are permitted to offer the blood as a sacrifice. You can drain the blood, pour the blood, and sprinkle the blood, but you can't eat or drink the blood because the life of that animal is in the blood. Likewise, you can't drink the blood of another human being, because the life of that human being is in the blood.

There were only four things that were carried over into

the New Testament which God forbade the people to continue to do. These four things, which are listed in Acts 15:29, are: 1) fornication, 2) abstaining from meats offered to idols, 3) eating things that were strangled while the blood was still in it, and 4) drinking blood. Jesus' listeners had therefore been forbidden to drink blood from childhood. Suddenly, Jesus came along and essentially said, "You must drink my blood or you won't have life." They were shocked and thought that Jesus couldn't possibly be speaking God's truth because He seemed to be saying something that was inconsistent with the Levitical law.

Was Jesus in fact saying something contrary to the Levitical law? No, He wasn't. He didn't come to contradict anything the Father had declared. He and the Father are one. Jesus came with the only kind of blood that was eternal and abundant and brought spiritual life. Human blood doesn't bring spiritual life, nor does animal blood. Only Jesus' blood brings spiritual life.

Jesus wasn't referring to physically ingesting or consuming His physical blood, but rather He was revealing a great spiritual truth. He was traversing the great chasm from the Old Covenant to the New Covenant. He was opening the windows of heaven and effectively saying, "I want you to rise above the fleshly realm now and embrace this spiritual truth." He was effectively saying that if, _spiritually_, you drink of His blood, you will have His life in you. Since spiritual life is sustained by spirit, there is no other way to sustain spiritual life. It cannot be sustained by natural life.

Many couldn't understand or accept what Jesus was saying, so they turned away from following Him. If they would have stayed with Him long enough, they would have come to understand His message, because at the Last Supper He took the cup and said, "This cup is the new testament in my blood." (I Corinthians 11:25) At that point, none of Jesus' physical blood had yet been spilled. He hadn't yet been crucified. He was speaking prophetically and spiritually about what was to come. He was also revealing to them the truth that just as cells, which are members of the human body, have "withdrawal privileges" of the life that is in the blood, we as people that are members of the spiritual Body of Christ likewise have withdrawal privileges from the life of God. In fact, we live at the mercy of the blood. Andrae Crouch communicated this truth powerfully in the lyrics of his great song which declared, "The blood that Jesus shed for me way back on Calvary; the blood that gives me strength from day to day will never lose its power."[1]

The Blood Gives Us Access and Withdrawal Privileges

The blood is a life-giving force. We can receive strength, health, and soundness of mind through the spiritual transportation system which is the blood of Jesus Christ.

Hebrews 10:19-22 communicates truth which relates to the important work that Jesus did and what it means to us as believers. Hebrews 10:19-22 declares, "Having therefore, brethren, boldness to enter into the holiest by the blood of Jesus, By a new and living way, which he hath consecrated for us, through the veil, that is to say, his flesh; And having an high priest over the house of God; Let us draw near with a true heart in full assurance of faith, having our hearts sprinkled from an evil conscience, and our bodies washed with pure water." In this passage, the writer is addressing "brethren," referring to people who are born again and are therefore part of the Body of Christ. He declares that we can have boldness to "to enter into the holiest by the blood of Jesus." The phrase "the holiest" refers to "the holiest of holies," which is representative of the presence of God.

This scripture shows us that the blood of Jesus gives us the privilege of withdrawing from the entire bank "in the holiest of holies," the presence of God, and everything it represents. We have access to, and can "withdraw," the joy of the Lord, the love of the Lord, the peace of the Lord, the power of the Lord, the help of the Lord, the strength of the Lord, and everything that is available in His presence. Psalm 16:11 declares, "In thy presence is the fullness of joy, and at thy right hand are pleasures forevermore."

We are like little cells in the great spiritual Body of Christ. What gives us the withdrawal privileges? We are always in need of something. We need protection, strength, help, direction, peace, or joy. We are needy creatures. We have to "eat" certain things to live. The Holy Spirit helps us understand and discern what we need, and we hunger for it, just as the human body hungers for things that it needs for nutrition. In the spiritual body, the Holy Spirit prompts us, and we know what we need. We have a right to receive from God everything He is, and everything He's provided, because of the blood of Jesus Christ.

The Blood Brings Us God's Provision

All of the things that God has made available have been provided for us and brought to us only because of the blood of Jesus. We can't gain entrance into the Holiest of Holies without the blood. We would be on the outside looking on. I believe that God wants us to learn to apply the blood and thereby release His provision in our situation. We can apply the blood to our own personal lives, our homes, marriages, and children. We can apply the blood to situations that are difficult or perhaps even impossible for us to solve or understand. The blood is flowing, constantly granting us the privilege of drawing from God's provision.

I believe there is power in the blood. Sometimes people say, "Do you think someone can put a curse on you?" I am not fearful of any curse, witch, or demon. I refuse to walk in fear, because I walk under the blood. No hellish thing can get to me, because it can't get through the blood. Satan tries to frighten people so we'll compromise with the spirit of darkness, and we'll compromise with the work of evil. But when we walk under the power and the covering of the blood of Jesus Christ, there is protection. I don't think we have any idea of how often we have been spared from disaster because of the blood.

Until we look at a somewhat lifeless body, in which all of the members and limbs are intact but the mind isn't wholly functioning, we don't appreciate the soundness of mind God gives us. Soundness of mind comes from the blood. There is nothing of hell and darkness that can defeat and destroy the blood.

Jesus' response to the disciples' request of how to pray is recorded in Matthew 6:11-12. "Give us this day, our daily bread." (Give us our groceries and more). "Forgive us our debts." (Take away our garbage). We not only have garbage in our homes that the garbage truck needs to haul away, but we also have garbage in our lives that the blood of Jesus has to take away.

Total Provision!

I can imagine a little cell in my body, in fact all one hundred trillion of them, rejoicing that the blood is still flowing. The blood has not lost its power. The blood is still going to give me what I need. Jesus has purchased, and through His blood has provided, everything I will ever need. All I need to do is receive it as it comes by. In like manner, I can say, "Blood of Jesus, take my garbage. Please handle this for me, because I can't deal with it. Take away the smell of my garbage."

Jesus' provision is complete. That's why the enemy wants to remove the blood from our songs and sermons. If the blood is omitted from our preaching, all that remains is a powerless lecture. The next time you partake of the Lord's Table, I encourage you to believe God for every provision He has promised. Is there healing in the atonement? Absolutely, because of the blood. Is there deliverance? Absolutely, because of the blood. What do you need today? Do you need encouragement? Do you need strength, help, or direction? What do you need? As you hold the communion cup you must understand that it is symbolic. It is just ordinary fruit juice, but as you ingest it by faith, you are looking to the blood of Jesus by faith.

Everything in our relationship to Him is by faith. I believe He will provide for you everything that you need. You won't find it in the ways of the world. You won't find it in people, possessions, or pleasure. If you're looking to be fulfilled by these things, you're going to be disappointed. Fulfillment is only found in Jesus, and it comes through the blood. "It reaches to the highest mountain, and it flows to the lowest valley."[2] The blood of Jesus will reach you wherever you are, and it will bring _life_ to you!

CHAPTER 2

The Cleansing Blood

Chapter 7 of the Book of Revelation transports us into the future and gives us a snapshot of a glorious event in which we, as born again believers, will participate. This depicts the scene when the multitude of saints is gathered around the Lamb, Jesus Christ. Please note that the saints represent all born again believers; all of those who have accepted Jesus Christ as their Lord and Savior. It is significant that the saints are wearing white robes. The robes are not dirty, stained, or soiled. They are a whiter white than we have ever observed on this earth. The blood of Jesus produces this kind of dazzling white, this kind of purity, and this kind of cleansing.

Revelation 7:14 declares, "This multitude are they which came out of great tribulation and have washed their robes and made them white in the blood of the Lamb." It is difficult with our limited mental faculties to imagine what this moment is going to be like. Our finite human minds cannot completely grasp something as awe-inspiring as this scene. Try to picture a sea of people in dazzling white robes as far as your eye can see, all blessing, praising, and worshipping the Lamb in perfect unison. The Bible declares that the saints have washed their robes in the blood of the Lamb and made them white.

I recall as a young boy singing several hymns that conveyed that truth. For example, "There is a fountain filled with blood drawn from Emanuel's veins and sinners plunged beneath that flood lose all their guilty stains."[3] Another hymn's lyrics asked, "Are you washed in the blood, in the soul cleansing blood of the lamb? Are your garments spotless, are they white as snow, are you washed in the blood of the lamb?" [4] And another hymn declared, "The cleansing stream, I see, I see! I plunge and oh, it cleanseth me! Oh! Praise the Lord, it cleanseth me, It cleanseth me, yes, cleanseth me!" [5]

Blood Is a Cleansing Agent?

Normally, we don't think of blood as a cleansing agent. We think of soap, detergent, or bleach as cleansing agents. In fact, blood soils and stains. We try our best to wash blood stains out of garments and other fabrics. We wash blood *out*, we don't wash *with* blood.

However, the Bible declares that blood is a cleansing agent. Revelation 7:14 refers to "saints with their robes white, washed in the blood of the Lamb." I John 1:7 declares, "If we walk in the light as He is in the light we have fellowship one with another, and the blood of Jesus Christ God's son cleanseth us from all sin." I John 1:9 states, "If we confess our sin, He is faithful and just to forgive us our sin, and to cleanse us from all unrighteousness." Clearly the scriptures teach exactly what the afore-mentioned hymns have declared, that *the blood of Jesus is a cleansing agent.*

That seems paradoxical. It sounds contradictory and it doesn't seem to make sense. However, that is only because we are looking at it from the wrong perspective. We are looking at it from an _external_ perspective, when we should be looking at it from an _internal_ perspective. When blood is outside our bodies (external), it is not a cleansing agent, but when it is inside our bodies (internal), it is quite another story, and a fascinating one at that!

When God created us, He designed our human bodies in such a way that the organs and systems of our natural physical bodies are analogous to spiritual truths. We can learn spiritual truths and principles by studying the way things work in the natural realm, and the human body is a perfect example of that. Inside our bodies, our blood is an amazing and powerful cleansing agent!

Blood Pressure

You have likely had the experience of having your blood pressure checked. Usually a cuff is wrapped tightly around your arm and then it is pumped up with air. While it is being filled with air, the cuff tightens around your arm and the pressure makes your arm feel very tight and somewhat uncomfortable. After a few moments, the medical attendant releases the air in the cuff and you hear a hissing sound, and then you simply wait to learn your blood pressure reading.

Once, I performed an experiment in which I repeatedly moved my arm, hand, and fingers while in the pressurized cuff. It didn't feel too badly at first, but as I continued, I began to feel tightness and a greater discomfort. Soon thereafter, I experienced a shooting pain. As I continued to move my arm, the pain increased and became more intense until I wanted to scream in agony. Finally, I couldn't move my arm at all anymore. However, when the cuff pressure was released, my arm started to feel normal again within a few seconds. What happened? When the cuff pressure was released, the blood which had been stopped in the upper arm was free to flow down into my hand and fingers, and my muscles could move and function without pain.

When I used my muscles while the cuff was on and the blood flow to my lower arm was stopped, the cells in those muscles were taking oxygen from the blood and converting it to energy. As a result of that process, the cells were expelling a toxic waste product. This toxin was the by-product of the muscle-moving process. I could move my arm the first few times and it didn't bother me much, but the more I did it, the more it hurt. As I continued to move my lower arm, hand, and fingers while there was no blood flowing to them, toxins were building up in my lower arm and they could not be washed away. Eventually, I experienced excruciating pain and that part of my body became paralyzed. If the blood flow would not have been restored, my lower arm would have literally died because the toxins were not being expelled. However, as soon as the cuff pressure was released and the blood flowed again, the red corpuscles in the blood began to soak up the toxins and carry them away. The blood cleansed my arm of the deadly toxins.

Close to the Blood

God created our bodies such that every single cell of our body needs to be cleansed by the blood. We have about one hundred trillion cells in our body. Mathematically, a thousand is a large number. One thousand thousand is a million. One thousand million is a billion (that's nine zeroes). If you have a thousand billion, you have a trillion (that's *twelve* zeroes). We have a hundred trillion cells in our bodies! The Creator put us together with incredible precision, knowing that all one hundred trillion cells need to eliminate the toxic waste given off as each cell performs its function.

God designed the blood to flow through capillaries, which are extremely miniscule vessels located throughout our bodies. The width of a capillary is the equivalent to the width of one human hair. There is no cell in the human body that is further away from a capillary than the distance of the width of a human hair! Therefore, every cell, all one hundred trillion of them, is constantly in the presence of the blood. It is hard to imagine the vastness of the network of capillaries in our bodies. They go everywhere. What an incredible proof of divine design. Someone once said that believing in evolution is consistent with believing that the dictionary came into being as a result of an explosion in a printing factory.

The Blood is Essential

Every cell in our body is in close proximity to the blood. The blood is a necessity. As the blood flows through our body, the red blood cells absorb the toxins and poisons. The red cells deliver them to organs that will remove them from the body. If the toxins which our cells produce remain in our bodies, they can potentially kill us. We exhale carbon dioxide, which is a waste product, from our lungs. God has built filtering systems into the body such as the kidneys, liver, and spleen, because the very process of living, moving, and functioning produces waste and toxins. God provided a way to expel those things which could kill us. We need the blood!

The human body's systems are a beautiful parallel to spiritual truths. The blood sustains life in our body by carrying away the things that threaten the life of our body. The blood is essential. If the blood is cut off, we simply cannot live.

Carrying Away the Toxin of Sin

Understanding the function of the blood in our physical bodies will help us to understand lyrics such as:

- *"Oh the blood of Jesus, it washes white as snow."* [6]
- *"The cleansing stream I see I see; I plunge, and oh it cleanseth me."* [7]
- *"Are you washed in the blood of the lamb?"* [8]
- *"There is a fountain filled with blood drawn from Emanuel's veins and sinners plunge beneath that flood lose all their guilty stains."* [9]

What is the spiritual toxin in our lives? What is the waste? What is the poison that we deal with as humans? *It is sin!* We have all sinned, according to Romans 3:23. Sin is missing the mark, coming short of the glory of God. Sin is toxic. Sin is poison. When it gets into our spirit, into our being, it will kill us if we don't deal with it. Romans 6:23 declares that "the wages," meaning the result, the consequence, "of sin is death." Therefore, unless something intervenes, the consequence of sin is death. Sin kills!

Conviction and Condemnation

When I moved my arm while the cuff was on, I started to experience excruciating pain. Eventually, I could no longer move it. The spiritual counterpart of that is called conviction. Sometimes when we sin, we keep going for a little while and think, "Ha, God must not have seen that one. Apparently, God wasn't listening. I got away with one." However, we soon start feeling "not so good." Things that we come across in life seem to remind us of the sin we committed or are continuing to willfully commit. This is called *conviction*, and it is one of the most wonderful things God has given us. Don't ever ignore or deny conviction, because it is the pain that lets you know that there is poison that will kill you if you do not deal with it. It is very important to understand that conviction is distinctly different than *condemnation*. Conviction is from God, and while it identifies the sin, it also brings hope through the fact that sin can be forgiven. Conversely, condemnation is from the enemy and it points to judgment and brings hopelessness.

Condemnation says, "You messed up and now it's all over. There is no forgiveness for you. You will never escape from the shackles of your sin. You are condemned!" Conviction says, "Release the cuff. The blood wants to flow. Let the blood get

to you, the pain will go, and the blood will wash out the toxin."
Condemnation says, "Your arm is going to die and there is nothing you can do about it." Conviction says, "There is always hope
because of the blood!"

You Are Hurting Yourself!

A Biblical illustration of this truth is found in Jeremiah
7:18 which states, "The children gather wood, and the fathers
kindle the fire, and the women knead their dough to make cakes
to the queen of heaven and to pour out drink offerings unto
other gods." This was referring to the idolatry into which the
people had fallen. They were worshipping other gods. God goes
on to state their motive. "They want to provoke me to anger."
We must understand that idolatry provokes God to anger, and
idolatry is worshipping or serving _any_ god other than Him. This
doesn't just mean worshipping a graven image. It is referring to
putting _any_ person, thing, or system before Him.

The next verse is powerful. In it God declares, "Do they
provoke me to anger? Do they not provoke themselves to the
confusion of their own faces?" Sometimes we carry "toxins" that
we shouldn't be carrying, such as unforgiveness, pride, bitterness, or hatred, and we think that we're doing it against someone
else or against God. Most of us have become angry with God at
one time or another. Perhaps something didn't happen the way
we thought it should have happened. Perhaps a prayer wasn't
answered when or how we expected. Perhaps things didn't "work
out" and we became irritated at God. We may have had thoughts
such as "I don't believe the Bible anymore. Prayer doesn't work.
I wish my pastor would get off my back."

In this Scripture passage (Jeremiah Chapter 7), God effectively said that the need for our cleansing is not just to please
Him so that He looks at us and says, "Good boy" or "Good

girl." Sometimes we get the idea that God is like a stern school-teacher who is looking down on us, and if we are going to find favor with Him we better do this or do that. However, in Jeremiah 7:19, God effectively states, "When you're following in the ways of idolatry and you think that you're doing it against me, you are actually the one getting hurt. You are hurting <u>yourself</u>." *The very fact that God calls us to confession and repentance is not just to please Him; it's to keep us from dying.* The toxin, the poison called sin, will paralyze and kill us. He loves us so much that He brings conviction, the "pain in our arm," to reveal our own destructive sin to us. Conviction is an expression of His great love for us.

The Purpose of Pain

Pain in our physical bodies can be a positive thing. I am in no way implying that we should embrace disease or sickness, but God built the pain mechanism into our bodies to get our attention. Pain indicates that there is something amiss in our bodies. Remember that conviction is an expression of God's love. He knows that if sin continues in our hearts, and if you harbor or continue to embrace or tolerate it, it is poison and it will bring spiritual death.

For example, we don't forgive people because they ask to be forgiven, or because we are endorsing their actions. We forgive them because the poison of unforgiveness will bring death to us. We cannot afford to have unforgiveness in our lives. It is poison! God says if we want to be healthy, then forgive others. Do you think you will get someone to change their mind if you lie down and kick your feet and throw a tantrum? That's a poison—get rid of it. Do you think you are "getting back at someone" by holding a grudge against them? Someone once said, "Holding a grudge is like letting someone live rent-free in your head." Get rid of that poison of bitterness and unforgiveness! God's solution is this: His blood comes, conviction comes, pain comes, and we should then respond by saying, "We better do something about this."

Confess and Repent

What then can we do about the sin, the toxin, in our hearts? God says to confess it. We all know that's not as easy as it sounds! We usually try to figure out whose fault it is so that we can try to fix the blame on someone else.

There are many people that think, "If I can get away with this, if God doesn't see, if this, if that..." By taking on that attitude (tolerating sin), they are allowing poison into their body. We must get rid of the poison. I am thankful that the blood is flowing through my physical body to do exactly that! I am even more thankful in the spiritual sense that the blood of Jesus has not lost its power and that it is available and flowing today. Because of the blood of Jesus, no one need be poisoned by sin. First of all, we must confess and repent of our sin. I John 1:9 declares, "If we confess our sins, He is faithful and just to forgive us our sins and to cleanse us from all unrighteousness." God can't forgive until we confess. When we confess our sins, the blood starts to flow, and the blood is a cleansing agent. Psalm 103:12 declares, "As far as the east is from the west, so far hath he removed our transgressions from us." Jeremiah 31:34 states, "I will forgive their iniquity, and I will remember their sin no more." Jesus' blood has picked up the toxin of our sins and removed it from our body.

Repent means to literally turn one hundred eighty degrees and go in the other direction. When we repent, God forgives us. A precious friend of mine often says, "Keep short accounts." Don't let the toxins build up. Don't let the sun go down on your wrath. (Ephesians 4:26) In other words, "Mr. Cell, stay close to the capillary." I'm no further than the width of a hair away from the blood! If we say what we shouldn't say or do what we shouldn't do, or in some other way miss the mark, we must immediately approach God in repentance—right then, right where we are—and acknowledge it to Him. As we do that and call on the name of the Lord Jesus, the blood will be released for our forgiveness and cleansing. The "cuff" will be released, and the blood will flow and carry away the toxin. We are saints with whitened robes because of the blood, not because of our record of good deeds, accomplishments, successes, or human efforts. We are saints <u>only</u> because of the blood of Jesus, which cleanses our bodies, souls and spirits.

Thankful for the Blood

There are three names given to the church, the people of God, in Scripture: the building, the bride and the body. As born again believers, we are the Body of Christ, and God cleanses His Body with His blood just like He created our physical bodies to be cleansed by our physical blood.

Thank you Lord for the sensation of pain in our physical bodies, because it calls our attention to the need for blood. Our bodies can only function properly when our cells receive blood. Our muscles can only relax and tighten as our cells are nourished with blood. Every time we move, our bodies produce toxins, waste, and poison, but <u>*at the same time*</u> the blood is flowing through us, absorbing the toxins and carrying them away. The blood cleanses us!

Thank you Lord for conviction, which calls our attention to sin in our lives. We are grateful that you show us where we have sinned so that we can deal with that deadly "toxin." Thank you for providing the cleansing stream, the blood of Jesus, to carry away our toxic sin and provide cleansing for us. Oh, the blood of Jesus, it washes white as snow! [10]

CHAPTER 3

The Overcoming Blood

As we serve the Lord and walk with Him, we encounter obstacles, opposition, persecution, and forces that are set against us to discourage us or interrupt our progress toward becoming all that God has intended for us to be. We must understand that we are in conflict, in warfare. Not only is there opposition coming against us, but there is also distraction. I John 2:16 speaks of the lust of the eyes, the lust of the flesh and the pride of life, all of which come to distract us. The enemy is here to try to defeat us. The spiritual valleys, wide rivers, and high mountains of life are here to discourage us. However, all of these things that comprise the enemy's strategy are subservient to the power of God and His Word. These things are not greater, stronger, or more powerful than the living God.

Conflict and Warfare

Sometimes people say, "I never have any conflict or warfare in my life." To me, that implies that they are not a significant threat to the kingdom of Satan, and consequently he is not very concerned about them. We must learn to embrace the warfare, as the Apostle Paul taught, because it is important in fulfilling God's purpose both personally and collectively.

Paul wrote in Ephesians 6:12, "We wrestle not against flesh and blood, but against principalities, against powers, against the rulers of the darkness of this world, against spiritual wickedness in high places." The Greek word translated "wrestle" refers to conflict or warfare. We are in a conflict against the forces of darkness and the power of the enemy. Paul wrote to his spiritual son Timothy and encouraged him to fight the good fight, to "wage the good warfare." (I Timothy 1:18 RSV) Paul wrote of his own personal testimony in II Timothy 4:7, "I have fought a good fight." It is abundantly clear from these Bible verses that *we are in conflict!*

The Weapons of Our Warfare

If we're warring and we are in conflict, then it is obvious that we have opposition. We have forces arrayed against us. Who then are we fighting? We must understand that it's not flesh and blood, not people nor personalities, which are our enemies. We are fighting the (spiritually dark) rulers of this world, spiritual darkness in high places, principalities, and powers. Our enemy is Satan, along with all of the fallen angels. Thank God that He has equipped us for battle. II Corinthians 10:4 declares that "the weapons of our warfare are not carnal, but mighty through God to the pulling down of strongholds." What are the weapons He has given us?

Revelation 12:11 speaks of two important weapons. John had a vision in which he saw Satan cast out of heaven, and in this verse, John called Satan by two names, the "accuser of the brethren" and the "deceiver of the world." Revelation 12:11 declares, "They overcame him by the blood of the Lamb, and the word of their testimony." The word "they" refers to the saints. The word "him" refers to Satan, the devil, the accuser of the brethren, the deceiver of the world. The saints overcame Satan by the blood of the Lamb and by the word of their testimony. The overcoming blood of the Lamb is an all-powerful weapon!

By observing the way God created our physical bodies, we can learn principles and truths that apply directly to the spiritual Body of Christ, which is comprised of all born again believers. I believe this will help us to better understand how we can overcome the enemy by the blood of the Lamb.

The Invisible Enemy

In the physical realm, we are totally surrounded by an inaudible, invisible, and powerful invading enemy. The power and force of this invisible enemy is responsible for a greater death toll than all of the wars, collectively, that have ever been fought. This very real enemy is present and at work in our physical bodies. I am referring to bacteria and viruses.

In the fourteenth century, an epidemic hit Europe which took the lives of one third of its population. In 1348 there were over a million people that took a religious pilgrimage to Rome, and while they were there, 90% of them became infected with a virus and ultimately died.

World War I claimed eight and a half million lives, but during the year of armistice when the great influenza epidemic hit, *twenty five million* people died. The flu claimed three times as many casualties as World War I! Sadly, my paternal grandfather was one of its victims. There was a time when the word "smallpox" struck terror in the hearts of people. Similarly, fear arose in people's hearts at the mention of polio and infantile paralysis, the virus that ultimately killed thousands of people. In recent decades, human immunodeficiency virus (HIV), which can lead to acquired immunodeficiency syndrome (AIDS), has exploded onto the world scene. AIDS is even more serious than any of the other viruses that have come before it for reasons which we will discuss later.

We are living in a world that is full of enemies. When we inhale, we are inhaling enemies. When we eat food with unwashed hands, we may be ingesting enemies. When we cut ourselves, these enemies can gain entrance into our bloodstream, and can threaten our very life. If we could see all of these invisible invaders, we would likely be terrified with the imminent threats all around us.

Soldiers in the Battle

However, God has designed our bodies to prepare us to stand against this enemy. Not only do we have natural defenses, but our bodies can in fact mount counter attacks so that when the enemies come against us we are not hopeless victims, but we have the means to overcome the enemies and be restored to health. When God designed us, He built an immune system into us. A critical part of our immune system is our circulatory system, which includes the blood that flows through our veins.

There are three primary "soldiers" in the battle that takes place constantly in our bodies. They are antigens, antibodies, and lymphocytes. The explanations contained herein are obviously an oversimplification of the lymphatic system, but please understand that this isn't intended to be a biology lesson but rather an attempt to uncover spiritual truth.

An _antigen_ is a chemical composition that has the potential to harm or destroy our body. Foreign material, viruses and bacteria are some examples of antigens. They are the enemies, the invaders, the silent attackers. Obviously, antigens are bad!

Antibodies are chemical compounds, proteins, which are produced in our body and have the capability to attack and to render the antigens powerless. Obviously, antibodies are good!

Lymphocytes are a specific type of white cell found in our blood. Twenty to fifty percent of the white cells in the average adult body are lymphocytes. Lymphocytes are very unique, important, and powerful, because they are our body's "security forces." They are the cells that identify the enemy and then "call out the good troops" to destroy the enemy.

Under Attack!

When we cut our hand, there is a probability that certain silent invading enemies gain entrance to our body through that wound. For the sake of simplification, let's call these invading enemies antigens. They have come to destroy and devour. When an attack takes place in our body, lymphocytes are moving about in our bloodstream. When we are well, there are about twenty five billion lymphocytes in our bloodstream and approximately another twenty five billion that are "loitering" in the vessel walls.

When an "enemy" infiltrates our body, the lymphocytes which are in motion detect the attack and send out a signal to the entire body, essentially saying, "We're being invaded. An enemy is attacking." Knowing that it has been invaded, the entire body immediately begins to respond. The capillaries dilate and the bone marrow begins to produce multitudes of white cells because it has been told that the body is under attack.

Identifying the Enemy

Identifying the enemy is a critically important early step. It is not enough to know that the body is under attack. The body must know *who* the enemy is in order to know *how* to fight. The lymphocytes begin to surround the antigen, pressing and pushing until they identify its shape and the manner in which it moves. They are continuously flowing back through the lymph nodes that are located in various parts of the body for the purpose of attempting to identify the invader.

For example, if the enemy is the measles virus, the lymphocytes find the formula stored in the lymph nodes. They look at it and say, "It's the measles virus." The lymphocytes then proceed to inform all the cells, "The enemy is the measles virus." The body then goes to work to produce billions of specific antibodies that attack the antigens, weaken them, and ultimately bring them to the point of powerlessness.

We need so many lymphocytes in our bodies because a given lymphocyte only has the ability to deal with one disease. A lymphocyte that understands and can identify measles is unable to identify any other disease. Each lymphocyte possesses its own unique intelligence. The more I learn about the human body, the more I am amazed by the incredible God we serve and the phenomenal way that He designed us. The lymphocytes call up troops to produce antibodies that will go to work to fight and destroy the specific enemy. Occasionally, however, an antigen can attack your body that the lymphocytes cannot identify. They simply don't know what it is. They check out all the stored formulas, repeatedly trying to identify it. They flow back to the lymph nodes and check down through the "database," but they can't identify it. The enemy is something new, something strange, something that can't be identified. The great epidemics in history occurred because viruses were introduced into a population in which certain blood types could not understand or identify a particular virus.

Timing is Critical

Timing is critical when an antigen attacks. The time period between the attack and the counterattack must be kept to a minimum, because while the body is trying to identify the antigen, the antigen is reproducing. In eight hours, it can reproduce a million more antigens. The interim time must be minimized so that the immune system can gather its forces and begin to fight back.

Antibiotics exist basically to provide some help during this time interval between the identification of the virus and the production of antibodies that will fight it. Antibiotics are not a solution or a replacement for the immune system. Antibiotics simply blast everything in sight, good and bad, but if even one antigen gets past the antibiotic, it will reproduce.

Immunization

The thing that is so horrible about the HIV virus is that it attacks the immune system, rendering it deficient and unable to produce the antibodies that are needed to counterattack the antigens. Doctors can pump antibiotics in repeatedly, and that may help to some extent, but it will never solve the problem because some of the bacteria will survive. The immune system is vital to our health. HIV is not just another virus. It literally targets the immune system—the very power of our body to keep us healthy. Isn't it like the enemy to attack our defenses and try to make us vulnerable? Instead of coming in the form of an antigen, he comes to destroy our ability to *identify* antigens, therefore rendering us ineffective to identify and destroy the invaders.

Immunization is a process that God allowed medical science to uncover, and it is the secret to dealing with the great epidemics that wiped out millions. It is also the secret to the healthy function of our bodies. Immunization can come in one of two forms—naturally acquired immunization, or artificially induced immunization.

Natural Immunization

The time immediately after a baby is born is the most vulnerable time in his or her whole life. The baby emerges from a very sterile uterus into a world that is full of germs. The baby has no ability in itself to fight germs because it has been in a sterile environment, but God has provided an incredible solution. Just before the baby is born, the placenta floods the bloodstream of the unborn baby and pours in all the antibodies that the mother has built up. For example, antibodies for smallpox, the mumps, chicken pox, and measles pour into the baby. Later, as the mother nurses the baby, more and more immunization is transferred to the baby. The baby therefore becomes equipped through the mother to be able to deal with a non-sterile world. The baby literally has borrowed antibodies. A baby receiving immunization from its mother is an example of naturally acquired immunization.

Another example of natural immunization is when a person has been through some particular illness or sickness and has overcome it. The lymphocytes have stored away the memory of that sickness. They carefully tucked it away and if it ever attacks again, they can immediately identify it and attack it. The more naturally acquired immunization a person has, the stronger and healthier they are, and the better they are able to cope with all the things that come against them.

Artificial Immunization

The other kind of immunization is called artificially induced immunization. Occasionally, we get sick and our body can't seem to overcome the antigen. Perhaps we begin to run a fever, get very ill, or lose our strength. One of two kinds of artificial immunization can be employed to counter such a situation. One is called *active artificial immunization*, and it involves injecting antigens that are either very weak or already dead from being in a fight in someone else's body. The purpose is to induce the body to produce antibodies to fight the invader.

Another method of immunization is called *passive artificial immunization*. In this process, the person is inoculated by the injection of antibodies, not antigens. These antibodies have come from a person that has already experienced the battle in their body and won. The antibodies were produced in another's body and the antibodies killed the antigens. The "victorious" antibodies are injected into another body, and the body can then identify the invading antigens and is able to produce more antibodies and go to war against the antigens and ultimately defeat them.

Throughout history, many great men and women dedicated their lives to understand and implement immunization, and we are the beneficiaries of their discoveries. We can be immunized against polio, measles, diphtheria, and whooping cough. After we are immunized against measles, for example, when measles tries to infiltrate our body, the lymphocytes quickly identify it because there are already measles antibodies in the bloodstream. The immune system is then able to produce billions more antibodies to fight, and win, the battle.

Dr. Paul Brand ministered in Vellore, India for a number of years, and gave an interesting account from his own personal life. *"Some years ago an epidemic of measles struck Vellore. One of my daughters had a severe attack. We knew she would recover, but our infant daughter, Estelle, was dangerously vulnerable because of her age. When the pediatrician explained our need for convalescent serum, word went around Vellore that the Brands needed the blood of an overcomer. We called for someone who had contracted measles and had overcome it. Serum from such a person would protect our little girl. It was no use finding somebody who had contracted chicken pox or recovered from a broken leg. Such people, albeit healthy, could not give the specific help that we needed to overcome measles. We needed someone who had experienced measles and had defeated that disease. We located such a person, withdrew some of his blood, injected the serum and, equipped with borrowed antibodies, our daughter fought off the disease successfully. She overcame measles not by her own resistance or her own vitality, but as a result of the battle that had taken place previously in somebody else."*

Sin is the Antigen

Let's apply this to the spiritual realm. <u>Sin</u> is the enemy that has attacked the spiritual well being of God's creation. In the Garden of Eden, sin attacked the spiritually healthy body of God's creation. Romans 3:23 declares "all have sinned and fallen short of the glory of God." <u>Death</u> is one of the consequences of sin's attack. Romans 6:23 declares, "the wages of sin is death." The end result and the consequence of sin is death.

Suddenly, this antigen called sin infiltrated God's creation. The human race, prior to that moment, was sterile, pure, and clean, and we could not deal with sin in and of ourselves. We still cannot deal with it on our own, because we do not have the antibodies in our spiritual being to fight sin. We are all born with a sinful nature (Ephesians 2:1). We are hopeless victims of sin unless there is an intervention.

Overcoming Sin

The human race was hopelessly headed for death, hell, and defeat because of the invasion of the antigen called sin. It was our (the human race's) fault that it came in, but God had a solution to our sin dilemma. God had a plan to send Someone that would live in the flesh and be exposed to all the antigens of the world, and yet be able to overcome every one.

II Corinthians 5:21 declares, "He hath made him to be sin for us, who knew no sin; that we might be made the righteousness of God in him." God the Father "made Jesus to be sin." The Father literally laid upon Jesus the "antigens" of the whole world while He was on the cross. During His earthly life, Jesus lived in the midst of all of the antigens of the world. Hebrews 4:15 declares, "for we have not an high priest which cannot be touched with the feeling of our infirmities; and was in all points tempted like as we are, yet without sin." *Jesus experienced every silent, invisible enemy that could ever destroy or bring death or defeat, and He overcame them all!* He was tempted in ALL points (He dealt with EVERY antigen), yet He was without sin (He identified and overcame EVERY antigen).

Hebrews 2:18 states, "For in that He himself hath suffered being tempted, He is able to succor them that are tempted." Because Jesus experienced every temptation and succumbed to none, He can come to our aid. He can be an inoculation for us against the antigen of sin. He can come to our defense because He has dealt with sin and defeated it!

Jesus Has Overcome the World!

The key is to find the person that has overcomer's blood! The key is to find the one that has already defeated what we are now facing. There is only one person that has defeated all the diseases, all the sin, all the iniquity, all of the viruses, and all of the bacteria. His name is Jesus.

In John 16:33, Jesus stated, "in the world ye shall have tribulation." The Greek word is *thlipsis,* which refers to trials, stress, pressure, or persecution. Jesus then went on to declare, "But be of good cheer, for I have overcome the world." Jesus lived here on the earth, stared the enemy in the face, stood nose to nose against him, and decisively defeated him. Jesus was effectively telling His disciples, "You need not worry because I have defeated sin and the enemy by my perfect sinless life of obedience to the Father." If you understand this great truth, it will make you free!

When Jesus died, perhaps the enemy thought, "I've vanquished Him! That's the end of the overcoming blood. I won't be threatened by those antibodies ever again. My little demon antigens have defeated Him." Wrong! Jesus rose from the dead to live forever. The Bible declares in Revelation 1:18 that He rose with the keys of hell and of death. We can interpret that as Jesus saying, "I've got the antibodies for hell and for death." That's why Paul could boldly declare in I Corinthians 15:55, "Oh death where is thy sting, oh grave where is thy victory?" As born again believers, death cannot defeat us because Jesus has given to us the antibody of eternal life.

Appropriating the Overcoming Work of Jesus

How do we appropriate the overcoming work of Jesus Christ? How do we get His antibodies into us? As we go through life, we encounter trials, problems, and needs. They may be physical, emotional, or spiritual issues. We encounter a problem and we try to wrestle with it, fight it, and deal with it. We do everything in our power, but we are unable to overcome it, because we can't manufacture the antibodies. The antibodies must come from one who has overcomer's blood, who has lived through it and defeated it. So how do we get the antibodies into us? We *plead the blood* and in doing so we appropriate the victory. Jesus has won by pleading the blood.

The word "plead" means to present or to argue a case. In a court of law, one party stands accused of wrongdoing and is called the defendant. Another party, called the plaintiff, brings the accusation and presents the prosecution's case against the defendant, who in turn presents a case for his defense. The defendant attempts to convey his position and persuade the judge and jury to agree with his position. The defendant literally pleads with the judge and jury.

Similarly, in the spiritual sense, pleading the blood is like saying, "I am standing against this thing that is coming against me and I am arguing with it." I am declaring to the antigens, "You are not going to win, because my spiritual lymphocytes have identified you. You're a liar. What you're telling me is not in line with the Word of God so you are a liar, because the Word of God will stand, though every man comes against it."

Sometimes our spiritual lymphocytes discern that certain information which is coming into our mind is a lie from the enemy. At that moment, we need to oppose it and overcome it. If we don't, it will keep growing and multiplying because it came from the enemy, who is called the father of lies. (John 8:44) The devil is a liar and a deceiver to his core. He will even lie about the lie! We cannot overcome him by reasoning with him or trying to declare our innocence based on our own merits. We _can_ overcome him by arguing our case—making our plea to the Father, the Righteous Judge—on the basis of the claims of Jesus' blood. The blood of Jesus remits our sin and when the Father hears "the blood" entered as a plea, he renders a "Not Guilty" verdict.

We must always argue our case solely based upon the claims of Jesus' blood and what He has accomplished. Spiritually speaking, we are immunized with the blood of an overcomer. Therefore, the enemy has to back away from us because the blood of Jesus is standing in our stead. We plead the blood! The enemy hates the blood. He's trying to take the blood out of every hymnbook and every sermon. You must know about and understand the blood, because it is the blood that carries the antibodies of Jesus, the overcomer.

The Angel of Death

Chapter 12 of Exodus describes the event of the passing of the Angel of Death over the land just before the children of Israel came out of Egypt. The homes in which the oldest child were spared were the ones who chose to apply the blood by smearing the blood of an innocent lamb on the doorposts of their home. The Angel of Death, that old "antigen," came by and said, "I can't take this one because they are living under the blood" so he went to the next house. That is the way it will work with you. Live under the blood of Jesus and the enemy will have no power over you. He'll say, "I can't touch this one."

We should understand this like never before as we see the analogy with the human body and how it functions. These song lyrics aren't just catchy little phrases, "There is power, power, wonder working power, in the precious blood of the Lamb."[11] That is truth! We could even modify the lyrics to say "There is power, power _overcoming_ power in the precious blood of the Lamb." I believe that's what John saw when he wrote in Revelation 12:11, "They overcame him by the blood of the Lamb."

Precious Blood

The blood of the Lamb is my justification (Romans 5:9), my redemption (Ephesians 1:7), and my victory (Revelation 12:11). The blood of the Lamb is my antibody. I _can_ overcome! I don't have to back off. I can stand and look at the enemy and say, "I will not fear. I will be bold. I will come against you in the name of Jesus (my authority) and by the blood of Jesus (my power)."

Peter called Jesus' blood "precious" in I Peter 1:19. It doesn't matter what we are facing or what we will ever face. When Jesus' blood flowed from the cross, it wasn't just liquid that fell on the ground. It contained powerful antibodies that were flowing for the whole world. No wonder the enemy shuddered! No wonder the enemy was upset! The demons, the little antigens, must have screamed, "If we would have known this would happen, we would never have crucified Him." (I Corinthians 2:8)

Next time you are faced with a threat, or fear starts to come upon you, plead the blood of Jesus. Say, "I plead the blood. I argue my cause on the basis of the claims of the blood of Jesus. That's where I'm standing and I'm not moving from that position. That's my defense."

Jesus' overcoming blood immunizes us with His spiritual antibodies so we can stand, not in our own strength, but in His. Not in our own power, but in His. That's what the Christian life is all about. It's not based on our works. It's based on appropriating His finished work.

Ask the Holy Spirit to help you to understand and apply this powerful truth. I believe God wants His people to walk in increasingly greater victory, but we will fail every time if we walk in our own strength. If we think we can out-strategize or out-manipulate the enemy, we're playing a losing game. We must boldly declare, "I'm walking under the blood." There is overcoming power in the blood of the Lamb!

CHAPTER 4

The Liberating Blood

Zechariah 13:1 declares, "In that day there shall be a fountain opened to the house of David and to the inhabitants of Jerusalem for sin and for uncleanness." The fountain that is opened is for "sin." The Hebrew word *chattath* is translated "sin" and it refers to all offense, all occasions of missing the mark. The fountain that is opened is also for "uncleanness." The Hebrew word *neddah* is translated "uncleanness," and it means rejection, separation, impurity, and filthiness. Zechariah's prophecy is declaring that there would be a fountain opened that would provide cleansing and restoration.

Zechariah 12:10 states, "And I will pour upon the house of David, and upon the inhabitants of Jerusalem the spirit of grace and of supplications and they shall look upon me whom they have pierced, And they shall mourn for him, as one mourned for his only son, and shall be in bitterness for him, as one that is in bitterness for his firstborn."

Both of the prophetic utterances above are referring to the Person and the work of our Lord Jesus Christ. They were prophetically pointing hundreds of years into the future, when Jesus would come to provide cleansing from sin, uncleanness and all manner of contamination to all who will believe and receive.

Amazing Medical Proof for the Purity of Jesus' Blood

In order for a fountain to cleanse, the contents of the fountain must be absolutely clean and pure. A contaminated or impure fountain cannot make something which is impure become pure. In order for Jesus' blood to cleanse, His blood had to be pure and uncontaminated. But how could that be possible since Jesus was born of a human mother?

Here is the fascinating truth of how God provided for Jesus' blood to be pure. We know and understand that in the human reproduction process, the egg of a woman is fertilized by the sperm of a man. The blood and its reproduction capability originates from the man. At conception, chemicals are produced in the uterus of the woman and a pouch-like organ is formed called the placenta. The fetus is connected to the placenta through the umbilical cord, which has tubes in it for incoming and outgoing blood. The fetus is separated from the mother's blood by the epithelial layers of the chorionic villae.

The circulation of the blood begins in the fertilized egg, which is called the embryo. _The blood of the fetus (baby) remains separate from the mother._ The food and waste material that are interchanged between the baby and the mother pass through the blood vessel walls from one circulation system to the other. The unborn baby does not receive its nourishment and oxygen from the mother's blood directly, but rather through the placenta.

The unborn baby's fetal heart pumps blood through the arteries of the umbilical cord into the placental vessels, which are imbedded in the uterine tissue. This procedure permits a diffusion of waste products through the placental walls from the child to the mother. It also permits nourishment and oxygen to flow through these walls from the mother to the child. This process is called osmosis. _There is no mingling of the two blood streams._ In other words, none of the mother's blood flows to the baby, and there is no fetal blood flow to the mother. Therefore, from the time the egg and sperm are joined at conception to the time the child is born, not one drop of the mother's blood mixes with the blood of the child. [12]

Therefore, it is a medically supported fact that although the baby Jesus gestated in the womb of Mary, *none of her blood mixed with His*. Since Jesus had no human biological father (He was conceived by the Holy Spirit), His blood was absolutely and altogether *pure*!

A Fountain Opened

The picture that we're given through the lips of the prophet Zechariah is that Jesus would come as a fountain. He would come containing pure blood, which is necessary to bring much needed healing, forgiveness, cleansing, peace, empowerment, redemption, sanctification, and justification. However, the work would not be complete until His blood was poured forth. Zechariah 12:10 declared that it would be poured forth by way of piercing. There would be an opening or openings made in His body, and the blood that was within Him would flow out and satisfy all of the requirements of redemption, sanctification, justification, peace, hope, help, and healing. *He would be as a fountain opened*.

Obviously, a fountain cannot provide its contents nor satisfy its purpose until it is opened. You can stand in front of a drinking fountain but it will not release its water until you press the bar marked PUSH. When you push the bar, out of that fountain will come the nourishment and refreshing that is necessary to satisfy your thirst. You can look at a drinking fountain all day and say, "Isn't that beautiful? Isn't that nicely mounted? Do you notice how the fountain shines because the chrome is polished? Do you notice it's located in a very convenient place?" You can make all of those observations but it hasn't satisfied its intended purpose until it is opened, which only happens when you hit the bar marked PUSH. Only then does it become "a fountain opened."

41

Zechariah prophetically states that Jesus must be opened (pierced) in order to become the fountain that would bring forth the benefits that His blood would provide. These benefits include justification, redemption, peace, cleansing, and sanctification. In order for us to receive these benefits, the blood that was in Jesus had to come out of Him so that it could be applied. He had to be pierced. He had to become "a fountain opened."

Pierced In Five Places by the Spirit of Grace

Zechariah 12:10 makes it clear that this ministry was done by the Spirit of Grace. The Spirit of Grace penetrated, punctured, and pierced Him. That is of particular significance, because in biblical numerology, grace is represented by the number five. Five is the "number of grace" in Scripture. The Spirit of Grace pierced Jesus in five places so that all of this provision could become ours.

The enemy thought he was destroying Jesus by crucifixion, but in fact he was unwittingly conforming to the plan of God, who by the Spirit of Grace was opening the fountain so that you and I could be redeemed, sanctified, justified, and cleansed, and so that we could have peace with God. While Jesus walked upon the earth, He revealed the Kingdom of God, but He could not bring sons into glory until He was pierced and His blood flowed. His blood had to flow as the only acceptable remission for sin.

We will examine the five places the Spirit of Grace pierced the fountain (Jesus), thereby opening the fountain for us.

His Back

The Spirit of Grace opened the fountain by piercing Jesus' back. Psalm 129:3, written hundreds of years before the time of Jesus, declares, "The plowers plowed upon my back: they made long their furrows." Isaiah 50:6 states prophetically about Jesus, "I gave my back to the smiters." When Jesus was brought to trial, part of the torture that He endured included a smiting of His back, a "plowing," if you will, of furrows upon His back that opened up the wounds from which His blood flowed. The Roman soldiers used an instrument called a flagellum to whip (scourge) Jesus. The flagellum was made of a short cylindrical wooden handle to which several strands of leather were attached. Sharp pieces of bone or metal were sewn at the end of each strand of leather.

The soldier that administered the scourging was called the lictor. He was a decorated Roman soldier that traveled with the magistrate. The soldiers would take the person that was being scourged and tie him to a post, binding his hands and exposing his back. The lictor would repeatedly swing the flagellum with all his strength, hitting the victim across the back and shoulders. On each stroke, the leather strands curled around the body and the sharp bits of bone and metal ripped the flesh and caused hemorrhages on the back and chest. As a result, the flesh began to separate down the back, and after several blows, blood began to flow. The soldier was very strong, capable, and experienced, and he would hit his mark. The victim's back soon began to look like plowed furrows. The back would soon be covered with blood, a fountain that was opened. Many times, those that were scourged would pass out from the pain, go into shock, or even die. The Romans referred to this torture as "the halfway death."

Recorded in Isaiah 53:4-5, the prophet foretold this event when he declared, "surely He hath borne our griefs, and carried our sorrows: yet we did esteem him stricken, smitten of God, and afflicted. He was wounded for our transgressions, He was bruised for our iniquities: the chastisement of our peace was upon him: and with his stripes we are healed." Peter, who watched Jesus' scourging, picked up the spiritual importance of it when he wrote his first epistle a few years later. I Peter 2:4 declares, "By His stripes we are healed." What was happening in Jesus' torturous scourging? The Spirit of Grace was opening the fountain, and the blood which flowed out of Jesus' back was for our healing in every dimension of our lives—physical, spiritual and emotional. The wholeness of God was made available to us when the fountain was opened.

His Head

The Spirit of Grace opened the fountain in a second place. Matthew 27:29 states, "and when they had platted a crown of thorns, they placed it upon His head." The word platted means braided or twisted together. The thorn bushes in that geographic area contained thorns that were very sharp and about an inch and a half in length. The thorns secreted a painful and poisonous fluid when they were broken. The Bible declares that after the soldiers had platted this crown of thorns, they placed it upon Jesus' head. The scalp is one of the most vascular areas of the body, and the capillaries are so close to the surface that any wound produces a large amount of blood. In mockery the soldiers said, "You say you're a king. Then you should have a crown."

As the crown was forcefully pressed onto Jesus' head, the thorns released their stinging poison into His scalp, causing a tormenting itching and burning. The Spirit of Grace was piercing the fountain a second time. In the blood which flowed down over His brow and over His face and garment, there was another provision that the Father was making. The piercing of the fountain on the head around the brow was a prophetic promise of God's protection, care, and liberating power over our thought life, which is one of the most vulnerable places to enemy attack. The term "thought life" refers to our innermost thoughts. Doubts, fear, unbelief, and uncleanness often attack our thoughts. Is there any help? Is there any hope? Yes! Jesus willingly accepted the crown, and the resulting blood flow made provision for our thought life. Because of the blood that flowed from Jesus' head, we can be set free from oppression, confusion, madness, and worry. He has given us soundness of mind.

Genesis 3:18 declares that thorns first came into existence as a result of the curse from the fall. There were no thorns until the curse. Thorns represent fruitlessness, and they are evidence of the divine judgment on the ungodly.

It is interesting that travelers through the desert areas of the Middle East will surround themselves with thorny twigs if they are faced with sleeping in the open at night. They encircle themselves with thorns as a protection against the attack of the deadly rattlesnake. The rattlesnake has a very soft belly, and it will not crawl across thorns, because thorns will tear its belly open. In fact, birds who are enemies of the rattlesnake will actually gather thorns and build a circle around the snake if they find it sleeping. When the snake awakens, it knows it can't escape. It therefore injects its venom into itself and it dies. The serpent won't cross the thorns!

Likewise, the serpent (Satan) cannot cross the thorns which protect our thought life because of the blood that flowed from Jesus' crowned head. We need God's protection for our thought life. Satan tries to bring doubts, fears, questions, temptations, vile imaginations, and evil and unclean thoughts into our minds. If we don't claim the blood of Jesus as protection and help, we are vulnerable to the work of the enemy.

We must plead the blood of Jesus over our minds and fill our thoughts with the Word of God. We must study the Bible and meditate on it, letting it dwell richly in us. As the devil sees the blood of Jesus applied to our thought life, he flees because he doesn't want his vulnerability exposed. We can be free in our thought life!

His Hands

The Spirit of Grace opened the fountain in a third place. Psalm 22:16 declares, "...They have pierced my hands." Most theologians believe that the Roman spikes were about five inches in length and were actually driven into the hollow at the very top part of the wrist. They were likely not driven through the palm, but rather into the wrist, because it could carry the weight of the body as He hung on the cross. The Bible uses the word "hand" because the wrist is considered a part of the hand.

In Scripture, hands represent service. For the first thirty years of Jesus' earthy life, He used His hands in the field of carpentry, building and repairing. For His last three and a half years, Jesus used His hands to serve in ministry. With His hands, He healed the sick, raised the dead, broke bread, and lifted Peter from the water in the storm.

We often use our hands in ways that are self serving, self pleasing, and self preserving. Jesus' hands were pierced, and the fountain flowed once again. The fountain touches our lives and changes us from being people who are only concerned about ourselves—our own welfare, promotion, preservation, and esteem—into people that want to minister to others. Our hands become instruments through which the power and the glory of God can help others. Jesus was speaking prophetically about the Church when He said, "They shall lay hands on the sick, and they shall recover." (Mark 16:18)

Chapter 28 of the Book of Acts gives the account of the Apostle Paul's shipwreck on the Isle of Melita. The crewmen built a fire to warm and dry themselves from the cold and the dampness. A serpent came up out of the fire and bit Paul's hand. The serpent was trying to destroy the ministry that God had planned for Paul. Paul shook the serpent off into the fire and the barbarous men were amazed when he did not die. He stood there to be a living testimony for Jesus. Not only did Paul personally survive, but sometime later he laid his hands upon the ill father of the governor of the island, and the man was miraculously healed. Because of that healing, the whole island turned to Jesus Christ. What was the serpent trying to do? He was trying to cut off the ministry of Paul's hands.

The enemy will try to do the same to us. He will try to keep us from serving God and serving others. He will try to hinder us from fulfilling the ministry to which God has called us. The blood of Jesus, flowing from His hands, was shed so that we too would be free to love and serve God and people as Jesus did.

His Feet

The Spirit of Grace pierced Jesus in a fourth place. Psalm 22:16 states, "They have pierced...my feet." Normally, the Romans would slightly bend the knees of the victim and place the right foot on top of the left foot, and then drive the spike down through both feet. The knees had to be slightly bent so that the victim could push himself up a little in order to breathe while on the cross. Otherwise, the victim would die of suffocation very quickly, unable to get air into and out of his lungs.

In the piercing of the feet, I believe God was speaking of the sanctified lifestyle, which we often refer to as our "Christian walk." When we are born again, we shouldn't live the way we used to live. We shouldn't walk like we used to walk. Now we have purpose and meaning in our lives. Now we have a destiny.

It is different than when we wandered aimlessly through life without knowing that there is a divine purpose for being alive. As born again believers, we know that God orders our steps and directs our path. Psalm 37:23 declares that "The steps of a good man are ordered of the Lord." We could never be redirected nor understand even what it means to be led by the Spirit if the fountain hadn't been opened for our feet. We would still be doing our own thing, going our own way, and walking our own path. I believe there is none more miserable in the Christian community than someone who's been touched by God but is not living a life consistent with His Word.

His Side

The Spirit of Grace opened the fountain in a fifth place. John 19:34 states that "one of the soldiers with a spear pierced His side, and forthwith came there out blood and water." When the soldiers approached Jesus on the cross, they came to break His legs. They typically used a one inch by three inch piece of wood about four feet in length. A soldier would hit the crucified one's legs with the wood, breaking the bones. Why? After the crucified one had suffered a great deal, breaking the bones of his legs would cause the weight of his body to drop. As a result, the lungs were compressed and he would immediately suffocate. When the soldiers came to Jesus, they noted that He was already dead and so they set the board aside. They didn't need to break His legs. This was a fulfillment of an Old Testament prophecy (Psalm 34:20) which declared that none of the Messiah's bones would be broken.

Instead of breaking Jesus' legs, the soldiers took a spear and plunged it into His side to make certain that He was dead. The soldiers likely drove the spear between the fifth and the sixth ribs and directly into the heart. In the process, the spear punctured the pericardium, which is a sac-like organ that surrounds the heart. John 19:34 states that when Jesus' body was pierced with the spear, blood and water flowed out of His side.

The fact that blood and water flowed from the pericardium is very significant. Medical experts say that because blood and water were both present in the pericardium, it proves that Jesus did not die of suffocation as was typical of crucifixion victims. Instead, Jesus actually died from heart failure. Ponder that for a moment. *Jesus literally died from a broken heart.* His love, compassion, and commitment to the world literally broke His heart. When the soldiers pierced His side, the liquid that flowed gave evidence of the brokenness that had already occurred inside.

Because Jesus' heart was broken and His blood flowed, our hard hearts can be changed such that we are softened and we become compassionate. Consequently, we care for others unselfishly with unconditional love. Because His side was pierced, we can draw near to the heart of God. Jesus reconciled us to God on the cross. Because of Jesus' blood, we can enter into God's presence, draw near to His side, and hear His heartbeat.

You and I are alive today only because of Jesus' undying love, indescribable compassion, and incomparable concern. That same love, compassion, and care is extended to us today to meet our deepest needs and to make us whole.

A Fountain Filled With Blood

An old hymn beautifully describes the fountain being opened. The first verse of that song powerfully states, "There is a fountain filled with blood drawn from Emmanuel's veins, and sinners plunged beneath that flood lose all their guilty stains."[13] The dying repentant thief on the cross next to Jesus rejoiced to see the fountain that day. He said to Jesus, "Remember me when you come into your kingdom." Jesus replied, "This day you will be with me in paradise." The second verse of the hymn states, "The dying thief rejoiced to see that fountain in his day, and there have I, though vile as he, washed all my sins away."

The third verse declares, "Dear dying Lamb, Thy precious blood shall never lose its power, till all the ransom church of God be saved, to sin no more." The fourth verse states, "E'er since, by faith, I saw the stream Thy flowing wounds supply, redeeming love has been my theme and shall be till I die."

I believe that, until we get to heaven, we will never wholly appreciate and understand what God did for us at Calvary. When we fully understand, we will stand before the throne of God and worship Jesus, the Lamb upon the throne. If He had not been willing to be opened, to be pierced, He would have still remained the Son of God, but you and I would not be sons of God. But because He surrendered His back to the whip, His head to the thorns, His hands and feet to the nails, and His side to the spear, He poured out His precious blood and thereby provided eternal and abundant life to us. The opened fountain brings us forgiveness, healing, and liberty.

"There is a fountain filled with blood drawn from Emmanuel's veins, and sinners plunged beneath that flood lose all their guilty stains." [14]

CHAPTER 5

The Efficacy of the Blood

As we examine the efficacy of the blood of Jesus, please note that the word efficacy means "having power to accomplish what it's intended to do." In other words, intrinsic in the blood is the power to perform whatever is necessary. Power isn't something the blood *has*; power is something the blood *is*. Power is intrinsic. The word intrinsic means "the essence of its character and nature." For example, love isn't something God *has*; love is something God *is*. We cannot separate love from God. Likewise, we cannot separate power from the blood of Jesus. I believe that Andrae Crouch was scripturally correct when he wrote the lyrics, "The blood that Jesus shed for me...will never lose its power."[15] The blood cannot lose its power because power is intrinsic in the blood. When you have the blood, you have power. Its power can never be diminished nor exhausted.

I had the privilege of growing up in a Christian home, and I observed my mother's unwavering confidence in the power of the blood of Jesus. As I grew and began to study the Scriptures, I came to understand that her convictions and actions were consistent with Scripture. Specifically, there were two actions that she took with the blood. She *applied* the blood and *pleaded* the blood.

Applying the Blood
In Exodus 12, when the Passover was first instituted, God instructed His people to slay a lamb, take its blood, and apply it

to the lintel and the doorposts of their house, and the Angel of Death would pass over. He didn't instruct them to apply it to the threshold, because we should never walk on or dishonor the blood. He effectively said, "If you apply the blood to the lintel and door-posts, it is sufficient to cover you." They applied the blood.

This is a proactive and preemptive action. I recall that my mother would get up every morning, and in her prayer time, she would "apply the blood" over the entire family, over the house, over her marriage, etc. She would apply the blood over anything and everything she cared about. This is an example of the application of the blood. My mother was *applying* the blood.

Pleading the Blood

The other action, which is equally important, is *pleading* the blood. The word "plead" means to argue a case or position in a court of law. It has to do with jurisdiction. In the legal sense, to plead the blood is to argue the merits of the blood. While application of the blood is proactive, pleading is often reactive. For example, when an unexpected crisis suddenly arises, we can plead the blood, which is immediately effective against the enemy. I remember my mother doing that in times of crisis. I grew up hearing her say, "The blood, Jesus!" I recall a time we were driving home from church on icy roads, and my father lost control of the car. My mother screamed, "The blood, Jesus!" She was pleading the merits of the blood. Satan hates the blood. He's been thwarted by it. He's been defeated by it. His plan didn't work because of the blood. He will ultimately end up in the lake of fire because of the blood. He absolutely hates the blood.

The Mystery

In I Corinthians 2:7, the Apostle Paul wrote about the mystery of the wisdom of God. The Greek word translated "mystery" is an interesting word which refers to a spiritual truth that can be known only by revelation and yet never fully understood by the human mind. In verse 8 he wrote, "The princes of this world knew it not, for had they known it, they would not have crucified the Lord of glory." Paul was referring to the forces, principalities, and powers of darkness. They made a huge mistake when they crucified Jesus and shed His blood. If they had understood the power in the blood, they would never have shed Jesus' blood. Satan unwittingly played right into the plan of God when he spilled Jesus' blood.

We must understand that Jesus' blood is a mighty weapon. When the enemy comes to us and says, "Remember what you said the other day?" We respond, "The blood!" Satan says, "Remember when you messed up earlier in your life?" We respond, "The blood!" Satan says, "The reason why you're not what you ought to be is because years ago you did thus and so." We respond, "The blood," and he must cease. He cannot prevail, because the blood has already defeated him. It has ruined him and thwarted his destructive plan.

Cain and Abel

There is a beautiful illustration of this truth in the Bible. One of the principles in Biblical hermeneutics (a science of interpreting the Bible) is called "the law of first mention." This means that there is great significance attached to the first time that a topic or subject is mentioned in the Bible. Therefore, we closely examine the meaning and context of a topic's "first mention," and we use that as a basis of interpretation for every other time it is mentioned. The blood is first mentioned in the Book of Genesis.

Genesis 3:17-19 declares, "And unto Adam he said because thou hast hearkened unto the voice of thy wife, and hast eaten of the tree, of which I commanded thee, saying, Thou shall not eat of it; cursed is the ground for thy sake. In sorrow shalt thou eat of it all the days of thy life; Thorns also and thistles shall it bring forth to thee; and thou shalt eat the herb of the field; In the sweat of thy face shall thou eat bread, till thou return unto the ground; for out of it wast thou taken; for dust thou art, and unto dust shalt thou return." The curse of the ground is part of the curse which came about because of the fall (Adam and Eve's sin).

Genesis 4:1 states, "And Adam knew Eve his wife; and she conceived, and bare Cain, and said, I have gotten a man from the Lord." Eve said that her baby son was *from the Lord*. She didn't say that he was from Adam. He came *through* Adam but _from_ the Lord. That is important for us to understand as God places children in our care. Another translation provides even more insight because it states, "I have gotten a man of God." There is a prophetic tone in this statement because it is referring to the child's God-given purpose. She was essentially saying that she received not just a man that God *made*, but one that God had *ordained to accomplish a purpose.*

The enemy fights hard against our children because he sees within them the giftings, talents, abilities, and future anointing to be a man or woman of God. Psalm 127:3 declares, "Children are an heritage of the Lord; and the fruit of the womb is his reward." Not only do children come *from* God, but they are fashioned *by* Him for His purpose.

A Keeper and a Tiller

Genesis 4:2 declares, "And she again bare his brother Abel. And Abel was a keeper of sheep, but Cain was a tiller of the ground." Abel was a keeper of the sheep. The Hebrew word translated "keeper" means that Abel was a steward of the sheep. In other words, Abel was taking care of something he didn't create. He was given the responsibility of taking care of that which the Lord made.

"But <on the contrary> Cain was a tiller of the ground." The Hebrew word translated "tiller" literally means "one that is a slave to or a worshipper of." The Hebrew word implies that Cain was a slave to the ground, and a worshipper of the ground. Because the ground had been cursed by God, Cain was therefore a slave to, and a worshipper of, something that God had cursed (Genesis 3:17-19).

Genesis 4:3 states, "And in process of time it came to pass, that Cain brought of the fruit of the ground an offering unto the Lord." Can you imagine thinking for a moment that we could make God accept something He has already rejected, or that we can run to God thinking He will receive something He has already cursed? We can see how Cain is missing the mark here. Who does Cain think he is? Who do we think we are, thinking that we can force God to receive what He's already rejected? I'm not referring to people that have failed or are struggling to overcome. I'm referring to people that are smug in their own way and in their determination to do what they're going to do regardless of what God's Word says. That approach simply doesn't work. God had effectively said, "I won't receive that thing. I have cursed it. Why do you bring that cursed thing to me?"

An example of this is when we say to God, "I don't care what You think or say. I am going to do what I want to do." Many people are convinced that God is going to show them favor because of their works, but they are incorrect. Ephesians 2:8-9 declares, "For by grace are ye saved through faith; and that not of yourselves: it is the gift of God: Not of works, lest any man should boast." Every time we bring works before God as the basis for our salvation, we are effectively trying to get Him to accept what He has already rejected. Cain was doing this, effectively saying, "Here God, receive the fruit of that which you have already cursed."

Watch That Attitude!

Genesis 4:4-6 declares, "And Abel, he also brought of the firstlings of his flock and of the fat thereof. And the Lord had respect unto Abel and to his offering. But unto Cain and to his offering he had not respect. And Cain was very wroth, and his countenance fell. And the Lord said unto Cain, Why art thou wroth? And why is thy countenance fallen?" God accepted Abel's sacrifice but did not accept Cain's, so Cain quickly developed an attitude. God is watching our countenance, our attitude. We think we're going to do our own thing, but God sees our attitude. He effectively said, "Why the long face, Cain? What's your problem? Why are you angry? Why are you jealous of your brother? Cain, the issue is between you and me. It's not between you and your brother. If you will simply do what you ought to do, you will receive what your brother received."

The next verse, Genesis 4:7, amplifies this thought as God declares, "If thou doest well, shalt thou not be accepted? And if thou doest not well, sin lieth at the door. And unto thee shall be his desire, and thou shalt rule over him." God was effectively saying, "Cain, you don't have any right whatsoever to be jealous. I'm not a respecter of persons, but I am a respecter of principles. If you do what Abel did, you will get what Abel got."

We are a product of our choices. There was jealousy and envy between Cain and Abel. Cain was upset with Abel, but Cain should have been upset with himself, because he was playing with something that had been cursed. When you play with something that has been cursed, it prevents the breakthrough. God was speaking to him, trying to help him understand. I like the fact that God challenged him, and that God is so patient that He will even talk to someone with an attitude. God will be patient with us and He will give us an opportunity to repent, just as He did with Cain.

The Blame Game

Genesis 4:8 declares, "And Cain talked with Abel his brother; and it came to pass, when they were in the field that Cain rose up against Abel his brother, and slew him." Cain, instead of talking vertically to God, started dealing horizontally with Abel. Abel hadn't done anything to Cain. Cain was upset because Abel was receiving from God the favor that he desired. But God was saying, "Cain, if you do what Abel does, you'll get the favor Abel's getting. The problem is not with Abel; it is between you and Me." We must understand that if we fail to become everything God wants us to be, it's not someone else's fault. God is too wise to put our future in someone else's hands.

When Jesus went to the pool of Bethesda (John Chapter 5), He asked the lame man, "Wilt thou be made whole?" That would sound like a foolish question if we didn't know that God is all wisdom. In the Bible, whenever Jesus asked a question of someone, His purpose was not to obtain information, because Jesus never lacked information. The reason He asked questions was to reveal to people the thoughts of their own hearts. Sometimes we don't know what's in our heart. "The heart is deceitful above all things, and desperately wicked; who can know it?" (Jeremiah 17:9) Occasionally something may come out of our mouth and we wonder, "Where did that come from?" It came from our heart!

The lame man at Bethesda answered Jesus and said, and I paraphrase, "Now Jesus, here's the problem. Every time the waters are troubled I don't have any man to put me in." What he was really saying was, "It's _their_ fault." However, if it would have really been someone else's fault, Jesus could have assigned one of the disciples to stay there and put the man into the water the next time the waters were troubled. Jesus wanted this lame man, who was lying there for thirty eight years, to understand that his condition wasn't someone else's fault. Cain's situation was similar. God was trying to make Cain see that it wasn't Abel's fault. He was effectively saying, "Cain, you're trying to settle with Abel something that is between Me and you."

Genesis 4:9 states, "And the Lord said unto Cain, Where is Abel thy brother? And he said, I know not: Am I my brother's keeper?" It is interesting that Cain wouldn't slay a lamb, but he'd slay his brother. Cain was lying to God when he said, "I know not." Why didn't God simply destroy Cain immediately because he lied to Him? I believe He let Cain live so that He could show us the mystery of the blood.

The Blood Gives the Ground a Voice

Genesis 4:10 states, "And he said, What hast thou done? The voice of thy brother's blood crieth unto me from the ground." Cain killed Abel to silence him, but instead he actually made Abel louder, because when the blood of Abel hit the ground, it gave the ground a voice. The ground did not have a voice until then. The blood gave the ground a voice that could communicate with God, a voice that God would hear and to which He would respond. Something happened to the ground when the blood hit it.

Let's make some application of this truth. Genesis 3:19 declares, "From dust thou art, and unto dust thou shalt return." We are a fallen race—we are "the ground." Paul wrote to the Ephesian church (Ephesians 2:1) that prior to knowing Christ, we are dead in trespasses and sins, there is no life in us, no communication with God, and our spirits are dead. When we are born again, we are regenerated. The word regenerated means to be "alive again." "Re" means again, and "generate" means alive. Our spirits are made alive. When we are born into the world, we do not know God and we cannot communicate with God because we are spiritually dead.

However, two thousand years ago, Jesus' blood was shed, and it hit the ground. Again, _we_ are the ground. We are born again by the blood of the Lamb. His blood touches this ground, and this ground that had no voice suddenly has a voice. Our spirits are regenerated, and we are brought into communion with God. Communication is restored between God and us. We are no longer spiritually dead because the blood has touched the ground. The ground that didn't have a voice now has a voice. The ground that was under the curse is now covered with the blood. Hebrews 12:24 declares that "the blood of Jesus speaketh better things than the blood of Abel." Abel's blood was crying for vengeance, but the blood of Jesus cries for mercy. That's what's changed us—the "better blood." The blood of Jesus speaks from the ground.

If Satan would have known the consequences, He would have never killed Jesus. "Which if the princes of this world would've known, they would not have crucified the Son of God." (I Corinthians 2:8) Satan thought that he was silencing Jesus' voice. Instead, he opened up millions of voices all over the world. Jesus speaks; He's not silent. Jesus isn't preaching anymore as a man using His vocal chords here on earth, but He's preaching from "the ground" now. He's preaching through _us_! He has all of this ground that's been given a voice by the blood. We have something to say that God will hear. We have something to say that shakes the very pits of hell. That's why Satan hates the blood. He messed up!

We Have a Voice!

The only hope that Satan has now is to keep us ignorant of that truth. If we don't know what's happened to us, then we won't do what we have the opportunity to do. Satan has already lost the battle with Jesus, so he wants to keep us ignorant and uninformed. We have something to say. We have a word to speak. We have a life to live. We have a gift to give. We are important, because the blood of Jesus Christ has touched our lives and given us a voice and a message!

Genesis 4:12 declares, "When thou tillest the ground, it shall not henceforth yield unto thee her strength; a fugitive and a vagabond shalt thou be in the earth." Please note that it says "*when* thou tillest the ground," not "*if* thou tillest the ground." Satan, you had your way with me before the blood hit me. You were tilling my ground, and everything you planted seemed to come up. You planted all kinds of garbage in there, and it came up. There was nothing to prevent it. Thorns and thistles. That is the testimony of our pre-Christian life—thorns and thistles. Now Satan's coming back, but when he does, since the blood has touched the ground, it will not yield its strength. Satan, you will not get out of it what you did before. It may look like you are having your way; it may look for a season like you're planting thorns and thistles, but although you may get me down, you won't keep me down. Satan, your plan won't succeed, because this old ground doesn't yield to your tilling like it previously did. You are now dealing with the blood. We're learning how to apply and plead the blood. We're learning about the power that is in the blood. We're learning that this ground is not like it used to be.

Jesus, You didn't say I wouldn't be tempted. You didn't say Satan wouldn't come back. You said, "...*when* thou tillest the ground..." But there is victory! There is liberty!

My friends, be encouraged if you have loved ones, friends, brothers, sisters, or parents that aren't walking in the light of God's ways. Keep believing. Put your confidence in the blood of Jesus, because the enemy cannot be as effective as he once was now that the blood has fallen on the ground.

Jesus' Blood Changes Everything

Isaiah 54:17 declares, "No weapon that is formed against thee shall prosper." I wish it said that there will be no weapon *formed* against thee, but it says that no weapon shall *prosper.* That means that the weapon won't accomplish its destructive intent. Two thousand years ago, Jesus' blood changed everything. The demons of hell said, "Oh no, we messed up. We thought we were shutting Him up. We thought we were stopping Him."

I John 1:9 states, "If we confess our sins, he is faithful and just..." Jesus is faithful to the work of the blood. The shedding of His blood satisfied all the demands of justice. Therefore, "He is faithful and just to forgive us our sins and to cleanse us from all unrighteousness." He's not faithful because we deserve it. He's faithful to the blood. It saddens my heart that so many in the church world are eliminating the blood from their hymn books and their messages. The enemy doesn't want the message of the blood preached. He is fearful of its power.

In our own strength, we do not have the power to overcome and live victoriously in the face of all of the things that are coming against us in the world today. However, we have available to us the blood of the One who has already overcome the enemy. Jesus walked where we walk and He was tempted in every way that we are tempted, yet He was without sin. He has resisted, conquered, and defeated the enemy. Satan knows that! If we could only understand and act on what Satan knows, and come to the place that we are as convinced as Satan is about the power of Jesus' blood, we would experience true power! The power is intrinsic in the blood, because Jesus won the victory. The blood that gives us strength from day to day reaches to the highest mountain and to the lowest valley. It will never, never, never, ever lose its power!

CHAPTER 6

Applying the Blood of Jesus

My sincere and heartfelt prayer is that this book has helped you to understand the importance and the incredible power of the blood of Jesus Christ, and how it can literally change your life. If you are a born again Christian, I rejoice with you, and I encourage you to receive all of the benefits that His blood offers you as a "blood bought" believer. I pray that this book will help you to rise to a new level in God.

If you have not yet received Jesus Christ as your Lord and Savior, I pray that God, through His precious Holy Spirit, will draw you near to Him and reveal His incredible unconditional love for you. God has designed your body in such a way that the very life-blood that flows through you illustrates His love for you. Just as your blood brings life, nourishment, cleansing, and protection, the blood that Jesus shed on the cross brings the very same spiritual benefits to you.

You may wonder, "How does God's plan of salvation work, and what does it have to do with blood?"

God is perfect and pure. There is no darkness or sin in Him. He is completely holy, and completely innocent of any wrongdoing. Sin and imperfection cannot exist in His presence. Heaven is literally a perfect place, where there is no darkness, death, or sin. If any contamination enters into a perfect place, then that place cannot remain perfect and pure. Because we are imperfect and impure human beings, a way had to be made to purify us so that we could gain entrance into the perfection of God's presence, and into the perfect place He has reserved for us called heaven. Our contamination had to be washed away, eliminated, and totally removed.

An Innocent Sacrifice

When Adam and Eve sinned, the human race became impure and contaminated. The contamination had to be dealt with. God chose to do it by covering them with the skins of an innocent animal (Genesis 3:21). This innocent sinless creature had to pay with its life. Its blood was shed so that Adam and Eve's sin, shame, and nakedness would be "covered."

From that time, God established the principle that, *in order to cover sin, the innocent must die and blood must be shed. The blood of the innocent purifies the guilty.* When the blood of the innocent is applied to the guilty, then God, the Righteous Judge, accepts the sacrifice of the innocent one who died as a substitute for the guilty one, and He declares the guilty one to be innocent!

This principle is evident throughout the Old Testament, as God required animal sacrifices to be made and offered to Him as a way to *cover* the sins of the people. For centuries, innocent animals gave their lives, and their shed blood satisfied God's requirement for sin. However, the blood of animals could only *cover* sin. It was not powerful enough to actually *take away* the sin. There is only One, Jesus Christ, whose blood is perfect and pure enough to *once and for all take away sin*. Jesus died as an innocent sacrifice on the cross. His sacrifice satisfied the holy and just requirement of the Father, who demands innocence and perfection as the entry criteria for heaven. Jesus paid the price for you. You were bought with a price—Jesus paid with His life and shed his uncontaminated, incorruptible blood. Hebrews 9:22 declares that without the shedding of blood there is no remission of sin.

When you repent of your sin and receive Jesus Christ as your Savior, His blood is "applied" to your life, and your sins are erased in God's sight. When God the Father looks at you, He no longer sees your sin, but He instead sees Jesus' perfection. He no longer sees your guilt, but He instead sees Jesus' innocence. He declares you to be pure and innocent, because His Son's blood has taken away your sin.

Sacrifice is difficult and even ugly at times. It is neither pretty nor easy. We cannot glaze over, minimize, or glamorize what Jesus endured. We must see it for what it was—torture, murder, and the ultimate sacrifice. It was bloody and it was repulsive to look upon. Isaiah 52:14 states that Jesus was so disfigured from the beatings and torture that He didn't even look human. Jesus endured that unspeakable suffering, shed His blood profusely, and sacrificed His very life for us.

Eternal Life!

It was necessary for Jesus to bleed and die so that His shed blood would do its wonderful work on our behalf. Because He died, we no longer have to suffer spiritual death, which by definition is "separation from God." We don't have to be eternally separated from God in a place that is called hell. However, because God is perfect, and we are imperfect when we sin, we cannot be in God's holy presence when sin is present. Romans 6:23 declares that the wages of sin is death. Death (separation from God and His holy presence) is the "wage" that is received when human beings sin.

How then do we avoid spiritual death (eternal separation from God) since we are imperfect and sinful? The latter part of Romans 6:23 provides the wonderful solution, as it declares "the gift of God is <u>eternal life</u> through Jesus Christ our Lord." Just as the Angel of Death passed over the Israelites when God saw the blood on the doorposts (Exodus 12:13), spiritual death will pass over us when the blood of Jesus has been applied to our lives. We will NEVER die spiritually (we will NEVER be separated from God), but instead we will live forever with Him. We will be given the gift of eternal life!

In Romans 5:9, Paul wrote, "Much more now being justified by His blood, we shall be saved from wrath through Him." All those who accept Jesus Christ will not have to experience wrath. They will not have to be judged for their sin and live forever in a Godless eternity. They are not going to have to pay the price for their sin, because Jesus already paid the price.

I invite you to accept the incredible sacrifice that Jesus made for you. You will spend eternity somewhere—either heaven (in God's presence) or hell (separated from God's presence). It is your choice. No matter what you've done in the past, or how far from God you may feel right now, you can live in God's presence forever! Your invitation to a relationship with God and entrance into heaven has already been bought and paid for by the blood of Jesus. You simply have to repent of your sin and accept His gracious invitation.

The Most Important Prayer You Will Ever Pray

The exact words aren't important, but the sincerity of your heart is. Pray to God right now along these lines: "Jesus, I come to You just as I am. I acknowledge that I am a sinner, and I have fallen short in many ways. I believe that You created me and You love me. I believe that You shed Your blood and died on the cross for me as my Savior, and You rose from the dead to give me new life. I repent of my sins. I want to change my ways and live for You. Please forgive me and wash me clean with Your blood. Give me a new start in life and help me to please You and fulfill Your intended purpose for me here on the earth. Thank You for loving me, Father, and for giving me the incredible gift of eternal life and the privilege of spending eternity in heaven with You, where there will be no more tears, no more pain, no more sickness or disease, and no more death. I love you Jesus, and I surrender my life to You as my Lord. Thank You God, for saving my soul and coming to dwell in me. Draw me close to You and help me to grow closer to You each and every day. Amen."

If you prayed that prayer in the sincerity of your heart, you are a new person in Christ! You are born again. You have received and applied the cleansing, overcoming, life-giving, powerful blood of Jesus Christ! Life here on earth will never be perfect, but now that you have placed your life in God's hands and you have applied Jesus' blood to your life, He will be right by your side as you walk in a new, wonderful, personal relationship with Him. Make time to be with Him every day, spending time in prayer, Bible study, worship, and meditation. Get involved with a Bible-believing church and serve the Lord with all your heart. I believe that as you do these things, the power of the life-changing blood of Jesus will be so evident in your life that you cannot help but pour out His love to others. The blood of Jesus will _never_ lose its power!

END NOTES

I—"The Blood Will Never Lose Its Power", Words & Music: Andrae Crouch

2—Ibid.

3—"There is a Fountain Filled with Blood", Words: William Cowper, 1772, Music: "Cleansing Fountain" 19th Century American camp meeting tune

4—"Are You Washed in the Blood?", Words & Music: Elisha A. Hoffman, *Spiritual Songs for Gospel Meetings and the Sunday School* (Cleveland, Ohio: Barker & Smellie, 1878)

5—"The Cleansing Wave", Words: Phoebe Palmer, Music: Mrs. J.F. Knapp

6—"Oh the Blood of Jesus", Words & Music: Anonymous

7—"There is Power in the Blood", Words & Music: Lewis E. Jones, 1899

8—"Are You Washed in the Blood?", Words & Music: Elisha A. Hoffman, *Spiritual Songs for Gospel Meetings and the Sunday School* (Cleveland, Ohio: Barker & Smellie, 1878)

9—"There is a Fountain Filled with Blood", Words: William Cowper, 1772, Music: "Cleansing Fountain" 19th Century American camp meeting tune

10—"Oh the Blood of Jesus", Words & Music: Anonymous

11—"There is Power in the Blood", Words & Music: Lewis E. Jones, 1899

12—Scientific references can be found in the following books which verify there is no mixing of blood in utero: The American Medical Association, "Home Medical Encyclopedia." Vol. I, pages 446-448; "Howell's Textbook of Physiology," 2nd Edition, pages 885-886; "Nurse's Handbook of Obstetrics" by L. Zabriskie, R.N., 5th Edition, pages 75-82.

13—"There is a Fountain Filled with Blood", Words: William Cowper, 1772, Music: "Cleansing Fountain" 19th Century American camp meeting tune

14—Ibid.

15—"The Blood Will Never Lose Its Power", Words & Music: Andrae Crouch

BIBLIOGRAPHY

Brand, Dr. Paul and Yancey, Philip. In His Image. Zondervan 1987

Brand, Dr. Paul and Yancey, Philip. Fearfully and Wonderfully Made. Zondervan 1987

DeHaan, M.R. The Chemistry of the Blood. Zondervan 1983

Murray, Andrew. The Power of the Blood of Jesus. Whitaker House 1993

Keller, W. Phillip. A Layman Looks at the Lamb Of God. Bethany House 1982

Ratliff, J.D. Your Body and How it Works. Reader's Digest Press 1975

Cosgrove, Mark. The Amazing Body Human. Baker Publishing 1987

More Inspirational Books from
Pastor Leonard Gardner

Eight Principles of Abundant Living

In this inspiring and thought provoking book, Pastor Gardner examines each recorded miracle in the Book of John to uncover spiritual principles of abundant living which can lead you into a lifestyle of deep satisfaction, joy, fulfillment, and true happiness.

The Unfeigned Love of God

The Bible uses the word "unfeigned" to characterize the indescribable love of God. Unfeigned means "genuine, real, pure, not pretentious, and not hypocritical." This powerful book, derived from a series of sermons by Pastor Gardner, will help you understand, accept, and embrace the incredible love God seeks to lavish on you.

Walking Through the High and Hard Places

Life has its ups and downs. The key to a fulfilling life is learning to "walk through" whatever situation or circumstance you encounter, and to emerge victoriously! The spiritual principles you learn in this book will give you the strength to handle any circumstance in life!

The Work of the Potter's Hands

You are not alive by accident! Isaiah 64:8 declares that God is the potter, and we are the clay. This book examines seven types of Biblical pottery vessels and the process the potter uses to shape and repair vessels. Learn powerful life lessons and know your life is in the hands of a loving God who is forming you through life's experiences so that you "take shape" to fulfill your unique purpose.

Coming Soon from Pastor Leonard Gardner

Chosen to Follow Jesus
The Blood Covenant
Principles of Prayer
Like an Eagle
Greater Than the Gates
Hindrances to Spiritual Growth
Hearing God
The Planting of the Lord

Contact Pastor Gardner to:
• receive Pastor Gardner's free monthly newsletter;
• schedule him for a ministry meeting at your church;
• or order his books and other resources.

Liberating Word Ministries
Pastor Leonard Gardner
PO Box 380291
Clinton Township, MI 48038
Phone: (586) 216-3668
Fax: (586) 416-4658
lgardner@liberatingword.org

Made in the USA
San Bernardino, CA
20 April 2014